Tiger Talk
All About Me

My Body

Leon Read

W
FRANKLIN WATTS
LONDON • SYDNEY

Contents

Look out for Tiger on the pages of this book. Sometimes he is hiding.

We all have a body.

Body parts

Our bodies have a head, shoulders, knees and toes, and eyes and ears and a mouth and a nose!

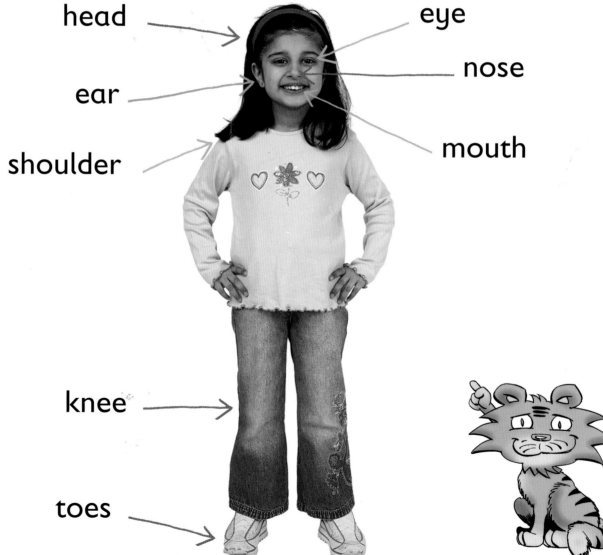

head

eye

nose

ear

mouth

shoulder

knee

toes

4

elbow

neck   finger

leg

foot

hair

arm

forehead

thigh

What other body parts can you think of?

5

Beautiful bodies

All of our bodies are different.

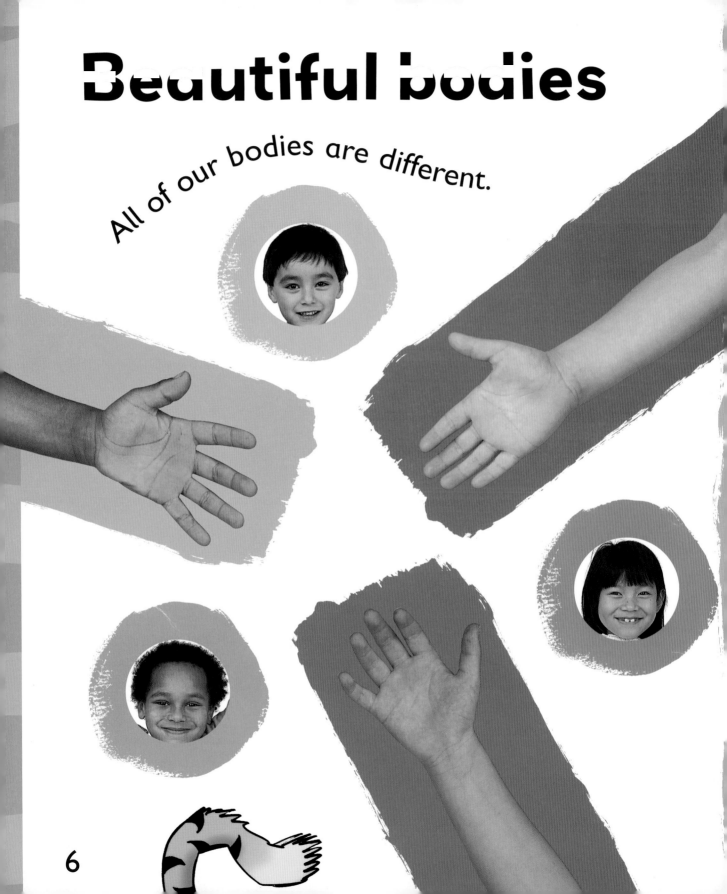

6

Use words like these
to describe your body.

brown eyes

black hair

round face

small ears

Using our body

We use our legs and feet to stand, walk, run, jump and dance.

Grace has a wheelchair to help her move around.

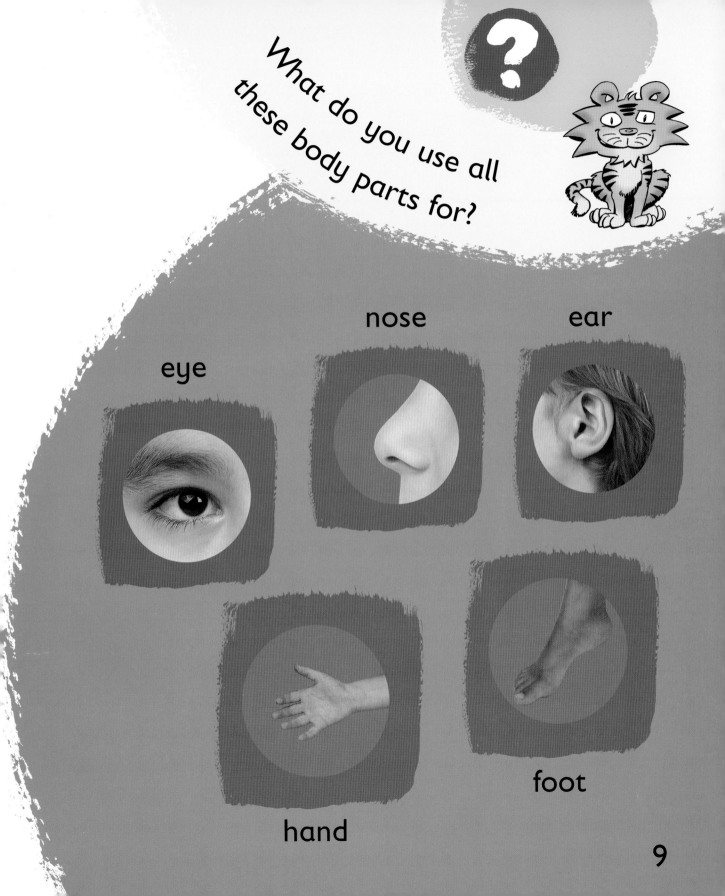

What do you use all these body parts for?

nose

ear

eye

hand

foot

9

Body energy

We eat food to give our body energy.

What happens if we do not eat?

My tummy rumbles!

I get tired and cross.

11

Quick and still

We are playing a game called statues.

Our bodies can move very quickly.

Our bodies can stand very still.

Copy Charlie

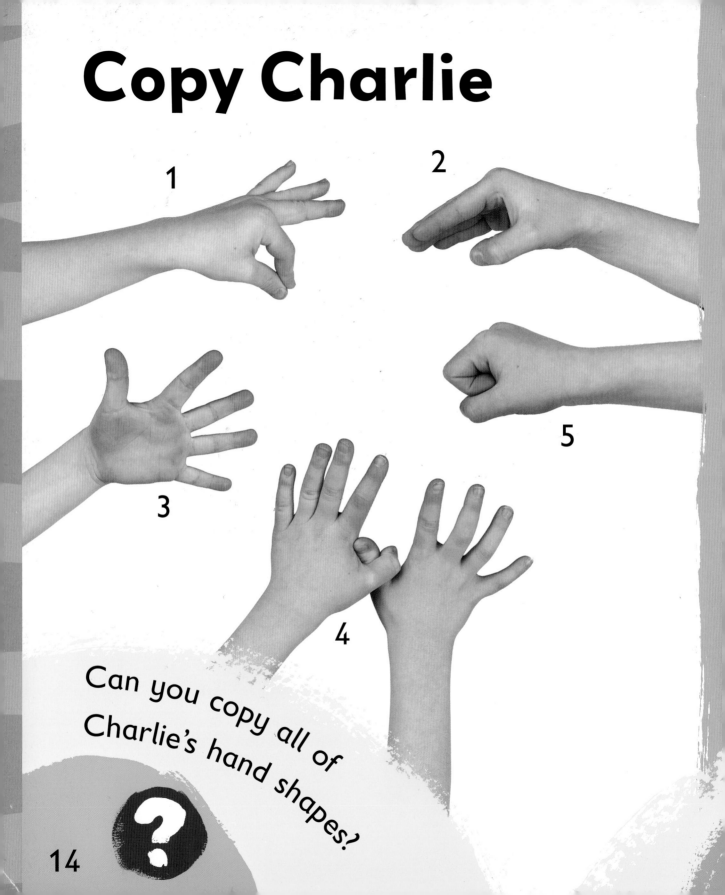

1

2

3

4

5

Can you copy all of Charlie's hand shapes?

?

1

2

3

4

Can you copy all of Charlie's body shapes?

?

15

Hairy head

We have hair on our head.

long hair

short hair

dark hair

blonde hair

When hair is cut, it grows back.

Why does my dad have a hairy face?

How tall are you?

Young people are not very tall.

I can't reach!

I'm taller than my best friend, but I'm shorter than my older sister.

Measure your family. Ask for help if you cannot reach. Who is tallest?

Ouch! That hurts

Falling over can hurt.

Ouch!

Billy has cut his knee.
I gave him a plaster.
It will help his knee
to get better.

All about me

Tiger has made a book about himself.

He included:  his height,

eye colour,

hair colour

and age.

Height: 20 cm.

Eyes: black.

Fur: white and orange

with black stripes.

Age: 4 years.

Look! I made a book and you can make one, too.

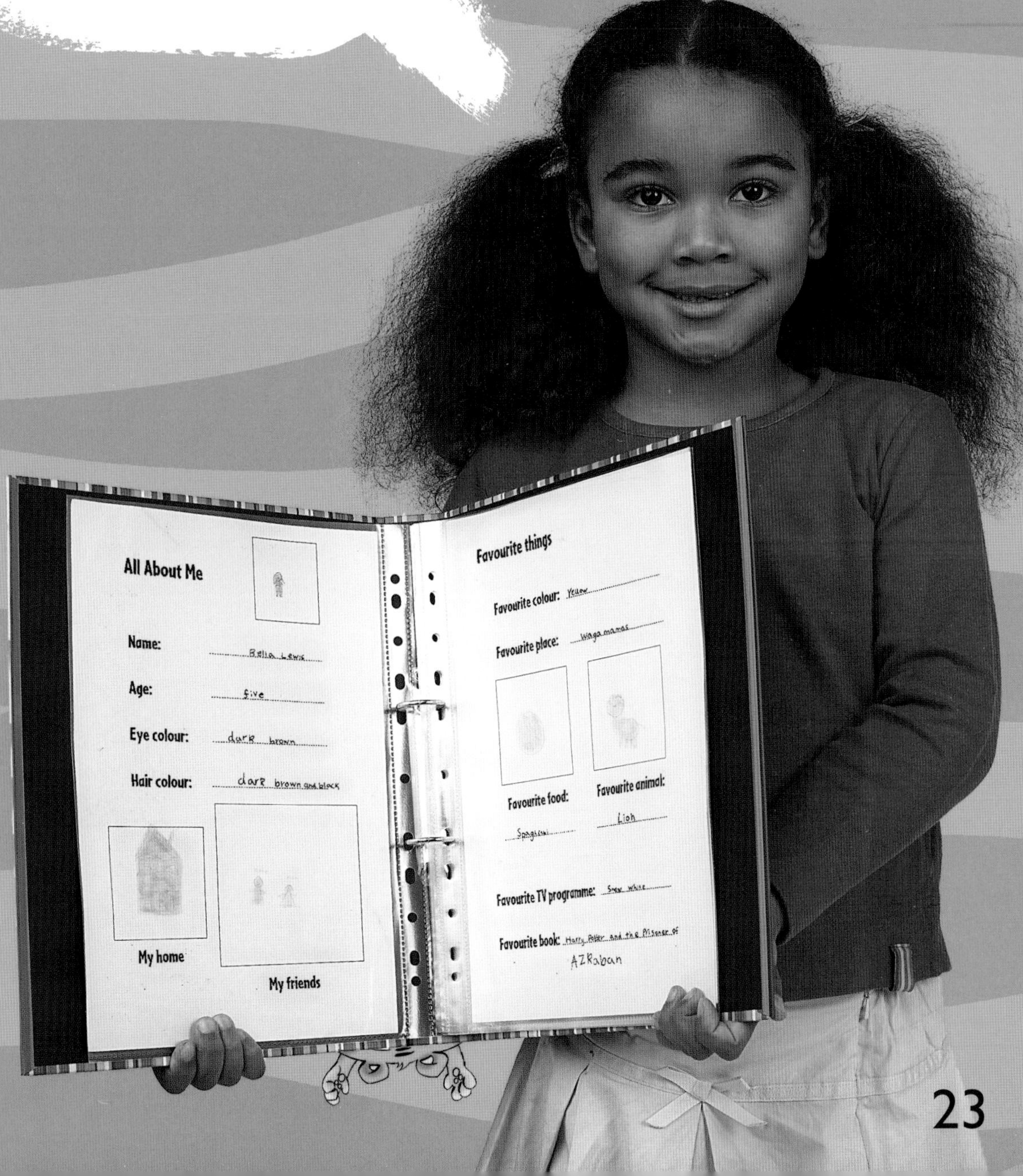

Word picture bank

Cut – P. 20

Eye – P. 4, 7, 9

Hair – P. 5, 7, 16, 17

Hand – P. 9, 14

Hungry – P. 11

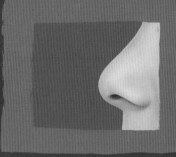

Nose – P. 4, 9

First published in 2007 by Franklin Watts
338 Euston Road, London NW1 3BH

Franklin Watts Australia
Level 17/207 Kent Street, Sydney NSW 2000

Copyright © Franklin Watts 2007

Series editor: Adrian Cole
Photographer: Andy Crawford (unless otherwise credited)
Design: Sphere Design Associates
Art director: Jonathan Hair
Consultants: Prue Goodwin and Karina Law

A CIP catalogue record for this book is available
from the British Library.

ISBN: 978 0 7496 7612 4

Dewey Classification: 612

Acknowledgements:
The Publisher would like to thank Norrie Carr model agency
and Scope. 'Tiger' puppet used with kind permission from
Ravensden PLC (www.ravensden.co.uk).
Tiger Talk logo drawn by Kevin Hopgood.

(17t) © Bohemian Nomad Picturemakers/Corbis.
(19) Lilly Dong/Botanica/Jupiter Images.

Every attempt has been made to clear copyright.
Should there be any inadvertent omission please
apply to the publisher for rectification.

Printed in China

Franklin Watts is a division of
Hachette Children's Books, an
Hachette Livre UK company.

There are 20 Tigers, including me, in this book.
Did you find all of us?

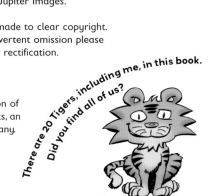